Seeley Brothers

Seeley Brothers

Manufacturers of Averill Paint, ready for use

Seeley Brothers

Seeley Brothers
Manufacturers of Averill Paint, ready for use

ISBN/EAN: 9783742833921

Manufactured in Europe, USA, Canada, Australia, Japa

Cover: Foto ©Thomas Meinert / pixelio.de

Manufactured and distributed by brebook publishing software
(www.brebook.com)

Seeley Brothers

Seeley Brothers

Offices:
NEW YORK,
  BOSTON,
CHICAGO.

SEELEY

BROTHERS

MANUFACTURERS OF

AVERILL PAINT,

READY FOR USE.

⇒✳AVERILL PAINT✳⇐

In submitting this book to our friends and the public, our object is to show the effect of different combinations of colors on the exterior of buildings.

*Within the limited space at our command we are only able to give a few Illustrations, sufficient, however, in connection with our **Sample Cards** and **Sample Boards**, to convey a fair impression of the effect of any of our colors when applied.*

*As we were the first to manufacture and introduce a **Paint ready for the brush**, we desire very briefly to refer to its origin and its influence upon the Paint Trade.*

*About twenty years ago **Mr. D. R. AVERILL** conceived the idea that a **Paint** prepared ready for use was not only practicable, but would also serve as a valuable contribution to the economic arts. Mr. Averill, being a practical chemist, with a large experience in the manufacture and manipulation of colors, began a series of experiments with a view of producing a practical **Mixed Paint**, which resulted in what is now known throughout the country as the **"AVERILL PAINT."***

*The first effort made to introduce it to the Trade was met by violent and virulent opposition on the part of Paint Manufacturers and Painters. Its advantages, however, in the matter of convenience, together with its superiority in point of durability, soon become apparent, and the formidable opposition organized to arrest its introduction yielded from necessity before convincing evidence. Wherever used it produced the most satisfactory results, and within a brief period found its way to nearly every town of any importance within the limits of our country. Manufacturers of the old style of Paints, realizing that the "new idea" was taking, and that the art of producing Paint was not altogether unprogressive, found it expedient to abandon their opposition to **Mixed Paint**, and at once began manufacturing it; and in face of their former assertions of its worthlessness, urged it upon the public with all the vehemence of new converts. They did not, however, cease their attacks upon the **"AVERILL."** They could not successfully oppose the introduction of **Prepared Paints**, but in order to introduce their own products, and because of the unparalleled success of the **"AVERILL,"** and the favor with which it was regarded by the public, they were not specially conscientious concerning the means they employed to injure* our business. Pamphlets containing mean insinuations were written and extensively circulated; salesmen were surcharged with vile epithets and slurs to be exploded on every favorable opportunity, until from temporary exhaustion they have called a halt for reinforcements. While it is not agreeable to our notion of mercantile dignity to refer disparagingly to our competitors or their products, we are nevertheless constrained to say that the course pursued by many manufacturers in characterizing the "AVERILL" has clearly demonstrated the utter littleness of human nature as found in the Paint Trade. The fact that the *AVERILL PAINT* has been on the market for nearly twenty years, being more extensively used than any other brand of **Mixed Paint**, and with a constantly increasing demand, ought to be, in connection with our ample guarantee, convincing proof of its superiority.

The growing desire of the American people to enhance the attractions of home in the way of exterior finish is quite apparent. To attain that which is most beautiful, and at the same time the most durable, is the legitimate object of those who study the art of exterior Painting.

The advances made in this respect since the introduction of the *AVERILL PAINT* are remarkable. Twenty years ago it was difficult to find a country house attractively Painted, the prevailing style being White with Green blinds; now many of our country houses are models of art and harmony as exhibited in the selection and arrangement of colors. This improvement has been accomplished through the medium of **Sample Cards**—first introduced by us—showing a variety of colors and shades, from which the house owner was enabled to study the effect of combinations, and from which he could make such selections as his taste approved. The House Painter has also, through the opportunity thus afforded improved his taste and been lifted out of the rut of prejudice and old-fashioned notions.

We desire to say, in conclusion, in connection with our remarks referring to our competitors, that it was with extreme reluctance we made any reference to their attacks. They have been so persistent, however, in their unfair methods, that we deemed it but justice to ourselves to say what we have. As a rule, we do not approve of noticing any uncomplimentary remarks concerning our goods, believing the public will not be influenced by such considerations.

Respectfully,

SEELEY BROTHERS,

BOSTON.   NEW YORK.   CHICAGO.

WEIGHT OF PAINT.

SOME of our competitors in the manufacture of Mixed Paint are unceasing in their attacks upon our goods, using among other arguments the fact that our product is *lighter in weight* than that made by them. This we concede. This argument, however, is either employed through ignorance or from a malicious desire to injure us.

Paint should not be heavy to produce a durable job. The opposite of this is true. It should be *light* in weight, containing only sufficient pigment to cover the surface, with as large a quantity of Oil as possible. The durable or wearing element of Paint is *Linseed Oil*. Pigments, except when in combination with Oil for painting purposes, possess no durability, and are used only to cover and beautify the surface; the Oil is to hold them, and constitutes the wearing and enduring property. Paint is readily made heavy by the use of a cheap pigment called "Barytes," and the object of its use is to deceive the purchaser and cheapen the product. This pigment is largely used as an *adulterant*, particularly by those most extravagant in their talk about *heavy* Paint and *pure* Paint, and if their goods are analyzed, they will be found to contain a large percentage of this useless and deleterious stuff.

Should any of our customers desire to have what is called a "heavy Paint," we will cheerfully manufacture it for them, and at a less price than we charge for the "AVERILL," provided they will order a sufficient quantity; but we will not *guarantee* it equal in quality for reasons before stated.

We simply desire to say to our friends, and to those who may be disposed to use our Paint: *First*, that we *guarantee* our goods to be equal, if not superior, to *any* Paint made. *Next*, that manufacturers who rely for the sale of their products upon their capacity to disparage the goods of their competitors are neither deserving of respect or confidence.

Respectfully,

SEELEY BROTHERS.

In offering to our friends the accompanying Illustrations, we have selected and arranged the colors in such combinations as, in our opinion, are best calculated to favorably impress the public, and have in most instances employed only new, popular and fashionable tints.

In doing so we are prompted by the demand for a change from the usual or common colors ordinarily used for body and trimming, and are simply following the present taste in House Painting. Fashions change in all things, and to conform to the various changes in taste is the necessity of both the Manufacturer and Dealer. The beauty and attractiveness of a house depends largely upon the colors selected for Painting, and the study in this art, together with the marked improvement in Architectural design of external construction during the past few years, calls for a departure from the old style of Painting, and have resulted in an improved taste in the selection of colors suitable and appropriate to the design of the structure.

These colors are manufactured from the best materials, and are **GUARANTEED** *to give satisfaction.*

Respectfully,

SEELEY BROTHERS,

Manufacturers of "The Averill Paint."

THESE SAMPLES ARE PAINTED FROM THE TANKS FROM WHICH OUR CUSTOMERS ARE DAILY SUPPLIED. SHOULD ANY SHADE BE DESIRED, NOT FOUND ON THE CARD, BY FORWARDING A SAMPLE OR DESIGNATING AS NEARLY AS POSSIBLE THE TINT OR COLOR, THE SAME WILL BE FURNISHED.

Nº 10	Nº 63	Nº 24	Nº 32	Nº 46
Nº 21	Nº 4	Nº 30	Nº 51	Nº 41
Nº 47	Nº 45	Nº 60	Nº 6	Nº 8
Nº 14	Nº 36	Nº 27	Nº 37	Nº 15
Nº 33	Nº 13	Nº 18	Nº 49	Nº 7
Nº 5	Nº 20	Nº 26	Nº 17	Nº 53
Nº 34	Nº 44	Nº 11	Nº 56	Nº 59
Nº 105	Nº 110	Nº 115	Nº 120

SEELEY BROT

MANUFACTUR

Rule for ascertaining the amount of Paint you require.

Add the number of feet in width [front and rear] to the number of feet in length [both sides]; this multiplied by the average height, gives the number of square feet to be painted. This divided by 200—as one gallon of this Paint covers 200 square feet, [two coats,] gives the amount required *in gallons*.

[EXAMPLE] Front, 20 feet.   120 feet.
       Rear, 20 "   [Multiply] Height, 20 "
       Side, 40 "
       Side, 40 "   200)2400

       120 "   12 gallons for two coats.

REMARKS.—There can be no definite rule established as to the exact quantity it will require; but the above is sufficiently near for all practical purposes. Should the surface be smooth and hard, *less* than the above would suffice; if rough and po

Notwithstanding the assertions of others in the manufacture of Paints that *their* goods will cover a third or half more surface than any other, we assure the public that our Paint *will positively cover as much*—if not *more* surface—gallon for gallon, than any other known Paint.

PUT UP FOR SHIPMENT IN

Barrels of 30 to 50 Gallons.   Pails 2 and 3 Gallons.
     Half Barrels 20 to 25 Gallons.   Cans of 1 Gallon, 6 in a Case.
       Kegs 5, 10 to 15 Gallons.   Cans of 1/2 Gallons, 6 or 12 in a Case.

WHEN ORDERING PLEASE GIVE EXPLICIT SHIPPING DIRECTIONS.

GENERAL DIRECTIONS

1. Paint only in clear weather, and on dry surfaces.
2. Cover knots with shellac, and putty nail-holes before applying first or priming coat.
3. Stir the Paint thoroughly before using.
4. Put the Paint on smoothly with as little rubbing as possible, flowing it on like varnish.
5. Be sure first coat is thoroughly dry before applying the second.

As we designate our colors by NUMBERS, reference should be made to our PAINTED SAMPLE CARD, which will be found in the front part of this book.

Any discrepancy that may be visible in colors between the Plates and our Samples representing same, is the difference between PAINT ITSELF and the closest approximation which can be obtained with PRINTING INK, without however, materially changing the effect.

PLATE I.

BODY,	No. 15
TRIMMING,	No. 27
SASH, STRIPING AND BLINDS,	No. 60
ROOF,	No. 115
CRESTING,	No. 60

To produce a similar effect, Nos. 36 or 10 can be substituted for No. 15 as BODY COLOR, and Nos. 8, 24 or 47 for TRIMMING.

Other pleasing effects may be produced by using for BODY, No. 44; TRIMMING, No. 33; SASH, No. 5; ROOF, No. 105; Or, for BODY, No. 41; TRIMMING, No. 46; SASH, No. 60; ROOF, No. 115; CRESTING, Blue or Black.

Upon every package of the "AVERILL PAINT" will be found the following

GUARANTEE.

We guarantee the Paint in this package will prove satisfactory to the purchaser when applied according to directions. We do not mean a guarantee of satisfaction ONLY WHEN THE PAINT IS FIRST APPLIED—as any Paint is satisfactory when first applied—but our guarantee embraces a sufficient time to properly test its merit.

Our friends from whom this Paint may be purchased are authorized to protect this guarantee.

SEELEY BROTHERS,

Manufacturers.

As we designate our colors by NUMBERS, reference should be made to our PAINTED SAMPLE CARD, which will be found in the front part of this book.

Any discrepancy that may be visible in colors between the Plates and our Samples representing same, is the difference between PAINT ITSELF and the closest approximation which can be obtained with PRINTING INK, without however, materially changing the effect.

PLATE II.

UPPER BODY,	No. 53
LOWER BODY,	No. 60
UPPER TRIMMING,	No. 27
LOWER TRIMMING,	No. 6
ROOF,	No. 115

To produce a similar effect, Nos. 10 or 36 can be substituted for No. 53 as UPPER BODY COLOR, and Nos. 7 or 11 can be substituted for No. 60 as LOWER BODY COLOR.

Other pleasing effects may be produced by using for UPPER BODY, No. 44; LOWER BODY, No. 46; UPPER TRIMMING, No. 60; LOWER TRIMMING, No. 27; ROOF, No. 115; Or, for UPPER BODY, No. 6; LOWER BODY, No. 60; UPPER TRIMMING, No. 34; LOWER TRIMMING, No. 4; ROOF, No. 105.

Upon every package of the "AVERILL PAINT" will be found the following

GUARANTEE.

We guarantee the Paint in this package will prove satisfactory to the purchaser when applied according to directions. We do not mean a guarantee of satisfaction ONLY WHEN THE PAINT IS FIRST APPLIED—as any Paint is satisfactory when first applied—but our guarantee embraces a sufficient time to properly test its merit.

Our friends from whom this Paint may be purchased are authorized to protect this guarantee.

SEELEY BROTHERS,

Manufacturers,

As we designate our colors by NUMBERS, reference should be made to our PAINTED SAMPLE CARD, which will be found in the front part of this book.

Any discrepancy that may be visible in colors between the Plates and our Samples representing same, is the difference between PAINT ITSELF and the closest approximation which can be obtained with PRINTING INK, without however, materially changing the effect.

PLATE III.

BODY,	No. 4
TRIMMING,	No. 46
BLINDS,	No. 60
ROOF,	No. 115

To produce a similar effect, No. 52 can be substituted for No. 4 as BODY COLOR, and Nos. 54 or 60 for TRIMMING.

Other pleasing effects may be produced by using for BODY, No. 49; TRIMMING, No. 54; ROOF, No. 115; BLINDS, No. 26; Or, for BODY, No. 45; TRIMMING, White; ROOF, No. 105; BLINDS, No. 60; Or, for BODY, White, and for BLINDS, Green or No. 60.

Upon every package of the "AVERILL PAINT" will be found the following

GUARANTEE.

We guarantee the Paint in this package will prove satisfactory to the purchaser when applied according to directions. We do not mean a guarantee of satisfaction ONLY WHEN THE PAINT IS FIRST APPLIED—as any Paint is satisfactory when first applied—but our guarantee embraces a sufficient time to properly test its merit.

Our friends from whom this Paint may be purchased are authorized to protect this guarantee.

SEELEY BROTHERS.

Manufacturers.

As we designate our colors by NUMBERS, reference should be made to our PAINTED SAMPLE CARD, which will be found in the front part of this book.

Any discrepancy that may be visible in colors between the Plates and our Samples representing same, is the difference between PAINT ITSELF and the closest approximation which can be obtained with PRINTING INK, without however, materially changing the effect.

PLATE IV.

UPPER BODY,	No. 21
LOWER BODY,	No. 27
TRIMMING AND SHADING,	No. 53
ROOF,	No. 115
CRESTING,	No. 60

To produce a similar effect, Nos. 5, 7 or 11 can be substituted for No. 21 as Upper Body Color, and Nos. 8, 14 or 24 for Lower Body Color, and No. 40 for Trimming.

Other pleasing effects may be produced by using for Upper Body, No. 56; Lower Body, No. 34; Trimming, No. 60; Roof, No. 115; Cresting, No. 53; Or, for Upper Body, No. 17; Lower Body, No. 18; Trimming, No. 6; Roof, No. 105; Cresting, Black.

Upon every package of the "AVERILL PAINT" will be found the following

GUARANTEE.

We guarantee the Paint in this package will prove satisfactory to the purchaser when applied according to directions. We do not mean a guarantee of satisfaction ONLY WHEN THE PAINT IS FIRST APPLIED—as any Paint is satisfactory when first applied—but our guarantee embraces a sufficient time to properly test its merit.

Our friends from whom this Paint may be purchased are authorized to protect this guarantee.

SEELEY BROTHERS,

Manufacturers.

As we designate our colors by NUMBERS, *reference should be made to our* PAINTED SAMPLE CARD, *which will be found in the front part of this book.*

Any discrepancy that may be visible in colors between the Plates and our Samples representing same, is the difference between PAINT ITSELF *and the closest approximation which can be obtained with* PRINTING INK, *without however, materially changing the effect.*

PLATE V.

BODY,	No. 37
TRIMMING,	No. 18
SASH AND STRIPING,	No. 6
BLINDS, · · ·	No. 60
ROOF, ·	No. 105
CRESTING,	BLACK.

To produce a similar effect, No. 17 can be substituted for No. 37 as BODY COLOR, and No. 41 for TRIMMING.

Other pleasing effects may be produced by using for BODY, No. 15; TRIMMING, No. 24; BLINDS, No. 21; ROOF, No. 110; CRESTING, Red or Blue; Or, for BODY, No. 14; TRIMMING, No. 8; BLINDS, No. 60; SASH, No. 53; ROOF, No. 105; CRESTING, Blue or Black.

Upon every package of the "AVERILL PAINT" will be found the following

GUARANTEE.

We guarantee the Paint in this package will prove satisfactory to the purchaser when applied according to directions. We do not mean a guarantee of satisfaction ONLY WHEN THE PAINT IS FIRST APPLIED,—as any Paint is satisfactory when first applied—but our guarantee endurances a sufficient time to properly test its merit.

Our friends from whom this Paint may be purchased are authorized to protect this guarantee.

SEELEY BROTHERS.

Manufacturers.

SEELEY BROS. NEW YORK

BOSTON

CHICAGO.

As we designate our colors by NUMBERS, reference should be made to our PAINTED SAMPLE CARD, which will be found in the front part of this book.

Any discrepancy that may be visible in colors between the Plates and our Samples representing same, is the difference between PAINT ITSELF and the closest approximation which can be obtained with PRINTING INK, without however, materially changing the effect.

PLATE VI.

Body,	No. 56
Trimming,	No. 46
Sash and Striping,	No. 60
Roof,	No. 115
Cresting,	No. 60

To produce a similar effect, No. 20 can be substituted for No. 56 as Body Color, and No. 34 for Trimming.

Other pleasing effects may be produced by using for Body, No. 41; Trimming, No. 51; Sash, No. 21; Roof, No. 110; Cresting, Black; Or, for Body, Nos. 14 or 24; Trimming, Nos. 10 or 45; Sash, No. 60; Roof, 120; Cresting, No. 53 or Blue.

Upon every package of the "*AVERILL PAINT*" will be found the following

GUARANTEE.

We guarantee the Paint in this package will prove satisfactory to the purchaser when applied according to directions. We do not mean a guarantee of satisfaction ONLY WHEN THE PAINT IS FIRST APPLIED—as any Paint is satisfactory when first applied—but our guarantee embraces a sufficient time to properly test its merit.

Our friends from whom this Paint may be purchased are authorized to protect this guarantee.

SEELEY BROTHERS,

Manufacturers.

As we designate our colors by NUMBERS, reference should be made to our PAINTED SAMPLE CARD, which will be found in the front part of this book.

Any discrepancy that may be visible in colors between the Plates and our Samples representing same, is the difference between PAINT ITSELF and the closest approximation which can be obtained with PRINTING INK, without however, materially changing the effect.

PLATE VII.

BODY,	No. 60
TRIMMING,	No. 27
SASH AND STRIPING,	No. 53
ROOF,	No. 120
CRESTING,	No. 60

To produce a similar effect, Nos. 11 or 21 can be substituted for No. 60 as BODY COLOR, and Nos. 33 or 8 for TRIMMING; CRESTING, Blue.

Other pleasing effects may be produced by using for BODY, No. 18; TRIMMING, No. 37 or White; SASH, No. 21; ROOF, No. 105; CRESTING, No. 53 or Blue; Or, for BODY, No. 44; TRIMMING, No. 24; SASH, No. 21; ROOF, No. 105; CRESTING, Black.

Upon every package of the "AVERILL PAINT" will be found the following

GUARANTEE.

We guarantee the Paint in this package will prove satisfactory to the purchaser when applied according to directions. We do not mean a guarantee of satisfaction ONLY WHEN THE PAINT IS FIRST APPLIED—as any Paint is satisfactory when first applied—but our guarantee embraces a sufficient time to properly test its merit.

Our friends from whom this Paint may be purchased are authorized to protect this guarantee.

SEELEY BROTHERS,

Manufacturers.

As we designate our colors by NUMBERS, reference should be made to our PAINTED SAMPLE CARD, which will be found in the front part of this book.

Any discrepancy that may be visible in colors between the Plates and our Samples representing same, is the difference between PAINT ITSELF and the closest approximation which can be obtained with PRINTING INK, without however, materially changing the effect.

PLATE VIII.

UPPER BODY,	No. 15
LOWER BODY,	No. 6
TRIMMING,	No. 46
ROOF,	No. 105
CRESTING,	BLACK.

To produce a similar effect, Nos. 10 or 36 can be substituted for No. 15 as UPPER BODY COLOR, and Nos. 5 or 7 can be substituted for No. 6 as LOWER BODY COLOR.

Other pleasing effects may be produced by using for UPPER BODY, No. 45; LOWER BODY, No. 32; TRIMMING, No. 8; ROOF, No. 105; CRESTING, Black; Or, for UPPER BODY, No. 27; LOWER BODY, No. 5; TRIMMING, No. 53; ROOF, No. 105; CRESTING, Black.

Upon every package of the " AVERILL PAINT" will be found the following

GUARANTEE.

We guarantee the Paint in this package will prove satisfactory to the purchaser when applied according to directions. We do not mean a guarantee of satisfaction ONLY WHEN THE PAINT IS FIRST APPLIED—as any Paint is satisfactory when first applied—but our guarantee embraces a sufficient time to properly test its merit.

Our friends from whom this Paint may be purchased are authorized to protect this guarantee.

SEELEY BROTHERS,

Manufacturers.

As we designate our colors by **NUMBERS**, reference should be made to our **PAINTED SAMPLE CARD**, which will be found in the front part of this book.

Any discrepancy that may be visible in colors between the Plates and our Samples representing same, is the difference between **PAINT ITSELF** and the closest approximation which can be obtained with **PRINTING INK**, without however, materially changing the effect.

PLATE IX.

UPPER BODY,	No. 4
LOWER BODY,	No. 21
UPPER TRIMMING,	No. 41
LOWER TRIMMING,	No. 10
ROOF,	No. 115
CRESTING,	No. 60

To produce a similar effect, Nos. 32 or 10 can be substituted for No. 4 as UPPER BODY COLOR, and Nos. 7 or 11 can be substituted for No. 21 as LOWER BODY COLOR.

Other pleasing effects may be produced by using for UPPER BODY, No. 6; LOWER BODY, No. 34; UPPER TRIMMING, No. 27; LOWER TRIMMING, No. 10; ROOF, No. 120; CRESTING, Red; Or, for UPPER BODY, No. 105; LOWER BODY, No. 115; UPPER TRIMMING, No. 120; LOWER TRIMMING, No. 110; ROOF, No. 115; CRESTING, Red,

Upon every package of the *"AVERILL PAINT"* will be found the following

GUARANTEE.

We guarantee the Paint in this package will prove satisfactory to the purchaser when applied according to directions. We do not mean a guarantee of satisfaction ONLY WHEN THE PAINT IS FIRST APPLIED—as any Paint is satisfactory when first applied—but our guarantee embraces a sufficient time to properly test its merit.

Our friends from whom this Paint may be purchased are authorized to protect this guarantee.

SEELEY BROTHERS,

Manufacturers.

As we designate our colors by NUMBERS, reference should be made to our PAINTED SAMPLE CARD, which will be found in the front part of this book.

Any discrepancy that may be visible in colors between the Plates and our Samples representing same, is the difference between PAINT ITSELF and the closest approximation which can be obtained with PRINTING INK, without however, materially changing the effect.

PLATE X.

BODY,	No. 15
TRIMMING,	· No. 34
BRICKWORK,	No. 34
SASH AND STRIPING,	No. 60
ROOF, · ·	Nos. 115 AND 105

To produce a similar effect, Nos. 10 or 44 can be substituted for No. 15 as BODY COLOR, and Nos. 46 or 60 for TRIMMING.

Other pleasing effects may be produced by using for BODY, No. 36; TRIMMING, No. 27; BRICKWORK, No. 115; SASH AND STRIPING, No. 60; ROOF, Nos. 115 and 105; Or, for BODY, No. 4; TRIMMING, No. 34; BRICKWORK, No. 115; SASH AND STRIPING, No. 60; ROOF, Nos. 115 and 105; Or, for BODY, White, and for BLINDS, Green or No. 60.

Upon every package of the "AVERILL PAINT" will be found the following

GUARANTEE.

We guarantee the Paint in this package will prove satisfactory to the purchaser when applied according to directions. We do not mean a guarantee of satisfaction ONLY WHEN THE PAINT IS FIRST APPLIED—as any Paint is satisfactory when first applied—but our guarantee embraces a sufficient time to properly test its merit.

Our friends from whom this Paint may be purchased are authorized to protect this guarantee.

SEELEY BROTHERS.

Manufacturers.

SEELEY BROS
NEW YORK.
BOSTON.
CHICAGO.

As we designate our colors by NUMBERS, reference should be made to our PAINTED SAMPLE CARD, which will be found in the front part of this book.

Any discrepancy that may be visible in colors between the Plates and our Samples representing same, is the difference between PAINT ITSELF and the closest approximation which can be obtained with PRINTING INK, without however, materially changing the effect.

PLATE XI.

BODY,	No. 20
TRIMMING,	·· No. 46
SASH AND STRIPING,	No. 53
BLINDS, ·	No. 59
ROOF, ·	No. 105
CRESTING,	BLACK.

To produce a similar effect, Nos. 13 or 56 can be substituted for No. 20 as BODY COLOR, and Nos. 34 or 59 for TRIMMING.

Other pleasing effects may be produced by using for BODY, No. 32; TRIMMING, No. 59; SASH, No. 60; ROOF, No. 115; Or, for BODY, Nos. 17 or 63; TRIMMING, No. 44; SASH, No. 21; ROOF, No. 105; CRESTING, Red, Blue or Black.

Upon every package of the "AVERILL PAINT" will be found the following

GUARANTEE.

We guarantee the Paint in this package will prove satisfactory to the purchaser when applied according to directions. We do not mean a guarantee of satisfaction ONLY WHEN THE PAINT IS FIRST APPLIED —as any Paint is satisfactory when first applied—but our guarantee embraces a sufficient time to properly test its merit.

Our friends from whom this Paint may be purchased are authorized to protect this guarantee.

SEELEY BROTHERS.

Manufacturers.

SEELEY BROS. New York. Boston. Chicago.

As we designate our colors by NUMBERS, reference should be made to our PAINTED SAMPLE CARD, which will be found in the front part of this book.

Any discrepancy that may be visible in colors between the Plates and our Samples representing same, is the difference between PAINT ITSELF and the closest approximation which can be obtained with PRINTING INK, without however, materially changing the effect.

PLATE XII.

UPPER BODY,	No. 34
LOWER BODY,	No. 4
UPPER TRIMMING,	No. 37
LOWER TRIMMING,	No. 46
ROOF,	No. 105

To produce a similar effect, Nos. 41 or 59 can be substituted for No. 34 as UPPER BODY COLOR, and Nos. 32 or 6 can be substituted for No. 4 as LOWER BODY COLOR.

Other pleasing effects may be produced by using for UPPER BODY, No. 24; LOWER BODY, No. 45; UPPER TRIMMING, No. 6; LOWER TRIMMING, No. 60; ROOF, No. 105; Or, for UPPER BODY, No. 21; LOWER BODY, No. 32; UPPER TRIMMING, No. 13; LOWER TRIMMING, No. 34; ROOF, No. 115.

Upon every package of the "AVERILL PAINT" will be found the following

GUARANTEE.

We guarantee the Paint in this package will prove satisfactory to the purchaser when applied according to directions. We do not mean a guarantee of satisfaction ONLY WHEN THE PAINT IS FIRST APPLIED—as any Paint is satisfactory when first applied—but our guarantee embraces a sufficient time to properly test its merit.

Our friends from whom this Paint may be purchased are authorized to protect this guarantee.

SEELEY BROTHERS,

Manufacturers.

PLATE XIII.

BODY,	No. 56
TRIMMING,	No. 18
BLINDS,	No. 60
ROOF,	No. 120

To produce a similar effect, No. 44 can be substituted for No. 56 as BODY COLOR, and No. 18 for TRIMMING.

Other pleasing effects may be produced by using for BODY, No. 63; TRIMMING, No. 34; ROOF, No. 115; BLINDS, No. 60; Or, for BODY, Nos. 17 or 37; TRIMMING, No. 18; ROOF, No. 120; BLINDS, No. 21; Or, for BODY, White, and for BLINDS, Green or No. 60.

As we designate our colors by **NUMBERS**, reference should be made to our **PAINTED SAMPLE CARD**, which will be found in the front part of this book.

Any discrepancy that may be visible in colors between the Plates and our Samples representing same, is the difference between **PAINT ITSELF** and the closest approximation which can be obtained with **PRINTING INK**, without however, materially changing the effect.

PLATE XIV.

UPPER BODY,	·	No. 4
LOWER BODY,		No. 34
TRIMMING AND SHADING,		No. 24
ROOF, ·	· ·	No. 105
CRESTING,	·	BLACK.

To produce a similar effect, No. 32 can be substituted for No. 4 as UPPER BODY COLOR, and No. 46 as LOWER BODY COLOR, and Nos. 8 or 27 for TRIMMING.

Other pleasing effects may be produced by using for UPPER BODY, No. 44; LOWER BODY, No. 14; TRIMMING, No. 60; ROOF, No. 105; CRESTING, Black; Or, for UPPER BODY, No. 53; LOWER BODY, No. 21; TRIMMING, No. 47; ROOF, No. 115; CRESTING, Red.

Upon every package of the "*AVERILL PAINT*" will be found the following

GUARANTEE.

We guarantee the Paint in this package will prove satisfactory to the purchaser when applied according to directions. We do not mean a guarantee of satisfaction **ONLY WHEN THE PAINT IS FIRST APPLIED**—as any Paint is satisfactory when first applied—but our guarantee embraces a sufficient time to properly test its merit.

Our friends from whom this Paint may be purchased are authorized to protect this guarantee.

SEELEY BROTHERS.

Manufacturers.

As we designate our colors by NUMBERS, reference should be made to our PAINTED SAMPLE CARD, which will be found in the front part of this book.

Any discrepancy that may be visible in colors between the Plates and our Samples representing same, is the difference between PAINT ITSELF and the closest approximation which can be obtained with PRINTING INK, without however, materially changing the effect.

PLATE XV.

BODY, ·	No. 4
TRIMMING,	No. 60
SASH AND STRIPING,	No. 27
ROOF, · ·	No. 115
CRESTING,	No. 60

To produce a similar effect, No. 32 can be substituted for No. 4 as Body Color, and Nos. 21 or 46 for Trimming.

Other pleasing effects may be produced by using for Body, No. 13; Trimming, No. 46; Sash, No. 60; Roof, No. 115; Cresting, Red; Or, for Body, No. 53; Trimming, No. 21; Sash, No. 33; Roof, No. 110; Cresting, Red.

Upon every package of the "AVERILL PAINT" will be found the following

GUARANTEE.

We guarantee the Paint in this package will prove satisfactory to the purchaser when applied according to directions. We do not mean a guarantee of satisfaction ONLY WHEN THE PAINT IS FIRST APPLIED—as any Paint is satisfactory when first applied—but our guarantee embraces a sufficient time to properly test its merit.

Our friends from whom this Paint may be purchased are authorized to protect this guarantee.

SEELEY BROTHERS.

Manufacturers.

SEELEY BROS.

NEW YORK.

BOSTON.

CHICAGO.

As we designate our colors by NUMBERS, reference should be made to our PAINTED SAMPLE CARD, which will be found in the front part of this book.

Any discrepancy that may be visible in colors between the Plates and our Samples representing same, is the difference between PAINT ITSELF and the closest approximation which can be obtained with PRINTING INK, without however, materially changing the effect.

PLATE XVI.

BODY,	No. 63
TRIMMING,	No. 34
SASH AND STRIPING,	No. 53
ROOF,	No. 105
CRESTING,	BLACK.

To produce a similar effect, Nos. 17 or 49 can be substituted for No. 63 as BODY COLOR, and No. 44 for TRIMMING; CRESTING, Blue.

Other pleasing effects may be produced by using for BODY, No. 4; TRIMMING, No. 34; SASH, No. 60; ROOF, No. 115; CRESTING, Red; Or, for BODY, Nos. 13 or 20; TRIMMING, Nos. 18 or 46; SASH, No. 60; ROOF, No. 105; CRESTING, No. 10, Black or Blue.

Upon every package of the "AVERILL PAINT" will be found the following

GUARANTEE

We guarantee the Paint in this package will prove satisfactory to the purchaser when applied according to directions. We do not mean a guarantee of satisfaction ONLY WHEN THE PAINT IS FIRST APPLIED—as any Paint is satisfactory when first applied—but our guarantee embraces a sufficient time to properly test its merit.

Our friends from whom this Paint may be purchased are authorized to protect this guarantee,

SEELEY BROTHERS,

Manufacturers,

SEELEY BROS. NEW YORK. BOSTON. CHICAGO.

As we designate our colors by NUMBERS, reference should be made to our PAINTED SAMPLE CARD, which will be found in the front part of this book.

Any discrepancy that may be visible in colors between the Plates and our Samples representing same, is the difference between PAINT ITSELF and the closest approximation which can be obtained with PRINTING INK, without however, materially changing the effect.

PLATE XVII.

BODY,		No. 24
TRIMMING,		No. 10
SASH AND STRIPING,		No. 56
ROOF,		Nos. 115 AND 105
CRESTING,		BLACK.

To produce a similar effect, No. 14 can be substituted for No. 24 as BODY COLOR, No. 36 for TRIMMING and No. 20 for SASH.

Other pleasing effects may be produced by using for BODY, No. 6; TRIMMING, No. 46; SASH, No. 21; ROOF, Nos. 110 and 105; CRESTING, Black or Blue; Or, for BODY, No. 32; TRIMMING, No. 60; SASH, No. 53; ROOF, Nos. 115 and 105; CRESTING, Blue.

Upon every package of the "AVERILL PAINT" will be found the following

GUARANTEE.

We guarantee the Paint in this package will prove satisfactory to the purchaser when applied according to directions. We do not mean a guarantee of satisfaction ONLY WHEN THE PAINT IS FIRST APPLIED—as any Paint is satisfactory when first applied—but our guarantee embraces a sufficient time to properly test its merit.

Our friends from whom this Paint may be purchased are authorized to protect this guarantee.

SEELEY BROTHERS,

Manufacturers.

As we designate our colors by NUMBERS, reference should be made to our PAINTED SAMPLE CARD, which will be found in the front part of this book.

Any discrepancy that may be visible in colors between the Plates and our Samples representing same, is the difference between PAINT ITSELF and the closest approximation which can be obtained with PRINTING INK, without however, materially changing the effect.

PLATE XVIII.

UPPER BODY,	No. 21
LOWER BODY,	No. 27
TRIMMING,	No. 53
ROOF,	No. 115
CRESTING,	No. 60

To produce a similar effect, Nos. 7 or 11 can be substituted for No. 21 as UPPER BODY COLOR, and Nos. 8 or 24 can be substituted for No. 27 as LOWER BODY COLOR.

Other pleasing effects may be produced by using for UPPER BODY, No. 53; LOWER BODY, No. 60; TRIMMING, No. 47; ROOF, No. 115; CRESTING, Red; Or, for UPPER BODY, No. 10; LOWER BODY, No. 8; TRIMMING, No. 60; ROOF, No. 110; CRESTING, Red.

Upon every package of the "AVERILL PAINT" will be found the following

GUARANTEE.

We guarantee the Paint in this package will prove satisfactory to the purchaser when applied according to directions. We do not mean a guarantee of satisfaction ONLY WHEN THE PAINT IS FIRST APPLIED—as any Paint is satisfactory when first applied—but our guarantee embraces a sufficient time to properly test its merit.

Our friends from whom this Paint may be purchased are authorized to protect this guarantee.

SEELEY BROTHERS,
Manufacturers.

SEELEY BROS. — NEW YORK. BOSTON. — CHICAGO.

As we designate our colors by NUMBERS, reference should be made to our PAINTED SAMPLE CARD, which will be found in the front part of this book.

Any discrepancy that may be visible in colors between the Plates and our Samples representing same, is the difference between PAINT ITSELF and the closest approximation which can be obtained with PRINTING INK, without however, materially changing the effect.

PLATE XIX.

UPPER BODY,	No. 34
LOWER BODY,	No. 44
UPPER TRIMMING,	No. 53
LOWER TRIMMING,	No. 60
ROOF,	No. 105
CRESTING,	BLACK.

To produce a similar effect, No. 59 can be substituted for No. 34 as UPPER BODY COLOR, and No. 34 can be substituted for No. 44 as LOWER BODY COLOR.

Other pleasing effects may be produced by using for UPPER BODY, No. 44; LOWER BODY, No. 44; UPPER TRIMMING, No. 4; LOWER TRIMMING, No. 21; ROOF, No. 105; CRESTING, Black; Or, for UPPER BODY, No. 115; LOWER BODY, No. 105; UPPER TRIMMING, No. 119; LOWER TRIMMING, No. 120; ROOF, No. 105; CRESTING, Black.

Upon every package of the "AVERILL PAINT" will be found the following

GUARANTEE.

We guarantee the Paint in this package will prove satisfactory to the purchaser when applied according to directions. We do not mean a guarantee of satisfaction ONLY WHEN THE PAINT IS FIRST APPLIED—as any Paint is satisfactory when first applied—but our guarantee embraces a sufficient time to properly test its merit.

Our friends from whom this Paint may be purchased are authorized to protect this guarantee.

SEELEY BROTHERS,

Manufacturers.

As we designate our colors by NUMBERS, *reference should be made to our* PAINTED SAMPLE CARD, *which will be found in the front part of this book.*

Any discrepancy that may be visible in colors between the Plates and our Samples representing same, is the difference between PAINT ITSELF *and the closest approximation which can be obtained with* PRINTING INK, *without however, materially changing the effect.*

PLATE XX.

BODY,	No. 37
TRIMMING,	No. 60
BRICKWORK,	No. 115
SASH AND STRIPING,	No. 53
ROOF,	No. 110

To produce a similar effect, Nos. 17 or 51 can be substituted for No. 37 as BODY COLOR, and Nos. 21 or 11 for TRIMMING.

Other pleasing effects may be produced by using for BODY, No. 45; TRIMMING, No. 8; BRICKWORK, No. 115; SASH AND STRIPING, No. 60; ROOF, Nos. 105 and 115; Or, for BODY, No. 13; TRIMMING, No. 41; BRICKWORK, No. 105; SASH AND STRIPING, No. 4; ROOF, No. 105; Or, for BODY, White, and for BLENDS, Green or No. 60.

Upon every package of the "AVERILL PAINT" will be found the following

GUARANTEE.

We guarantee the Paint in this package will prove satisfactory to the purchaser when applied according to directions. We do not mean a guarantee of satisfaction ONLY WHEN THE PAINT IS FIRST APPLIED—*as any Paint is satisfactory when first applied—but our guarantee embraces a sufficient time to properly test its merit.*

Our friends from whom this Paint may be purchased are authorized to protect this guarantee.

SEELEY BROTHERS,

Manufacturer.

SEELEY BROS

NEW YORK.

BOSTON.

CHICAGO.

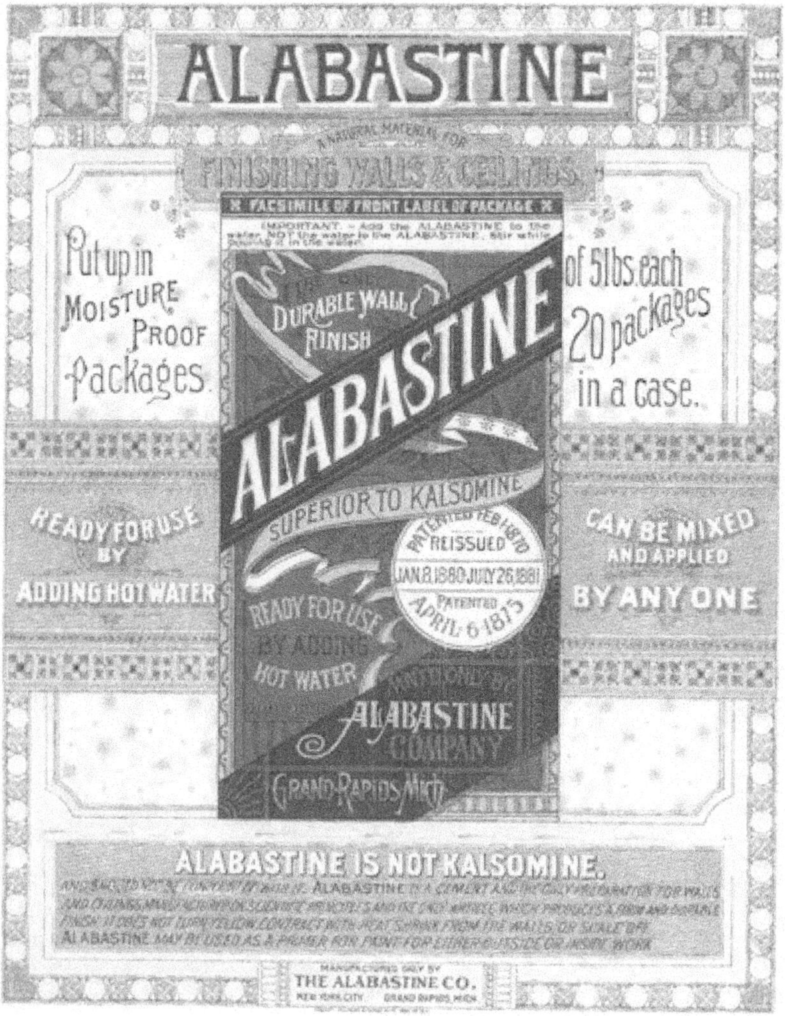

ALABASTINE
FINISHING WALLS & CEILINGS
FACSIMILE OF FRONT LABEL OF PACKAGE
Put up in MOISTURE PROOF Packages
of 5 lbs. each 20 packages in a case.
DURABLE WALL FINISH
ALABASTINE
SUPERIOR TO KALSOMINE
PATENTED FEB 1 1870
REISSUED
JAN. 8 1880 JULY 26, 1881
PATENTED APRIL 6 1875
READY FOR USE BY ADDING HOT WATER
ALABASTINE COMPANY
GRAND RAPIDS MICH
READY FOR USE BY ADDING HOT WATER
CAN BE MIXED AND APPLIED BY ANY ONE
ALABASTINE IS NOT KALSOMINE.
MANUFACTURED ONLY BY
THE ALABASTINE CO.
NEW YORK CITY
GRAND RAPIDS, MICH

ALABASTINE

SUPERIOR TO KALSOMINE.

CAN + BE + APPLIED + BY + ANYONE.

Its convenience and utility will be appreciated when it is considered that

ANY HOUSEKEEPER

can apply it, without the aid of skilled labor, and at a moderate cost.

ALABASTINE

Is an article designed for Walls and Ceilings, and is rapidly superseding all preparations usually employed for this purpose. The objections to the use of Whitewash and the ordinary Kalsomine, are so well known, that any reference to the subject is almost unnecessary.

ALABASTINE is a valuable discovery. It constitutes a *permanent* finish for Walls, assimilating with the plaster, *and will not rub off*. It does not deteriorate by age; in this respect it is unlike all other preparations of a similar character.

ALABASTINE is a *disinfectant*, and renders apartments healthful.

It is the only natural and durable material with which to finish Walls and Ceilings.

It is cheaper than Kalsomine; works easier, and may be applied by anyone. After cleaning, no sizing or other preparation for the Walls is necessary, and one coat can be applied upon another as soon as dry.

It is *whiter* than any other material, and the tints are more clear and more delicate. The White will not turn *yellow*, nor the tints *fade*.

Cracks in Walls can be easily filled with the brush and a little thick ALABASTINE, while applying the first coat. This cannot be done with Kalsomine.

ALABASTINE can be applied over *old* Kalsomine or Whitewash, which, however, should be washed or scraped off, to insure a first-class job.

It is the most suitable article for using over Wall Paper, or soiled painted Walls.

Wood Ceilings, whether painted or not, can be made *whiter* with one coat of ALABASTINE than with three coats of Lead or Zinc.

www.ingramcontent.com/pod-product-compliance
Lightning Source LLC
Chambersburg PA
CBHW030551270326
41927CB00008B/1594